ON BEING A SCULPTOR

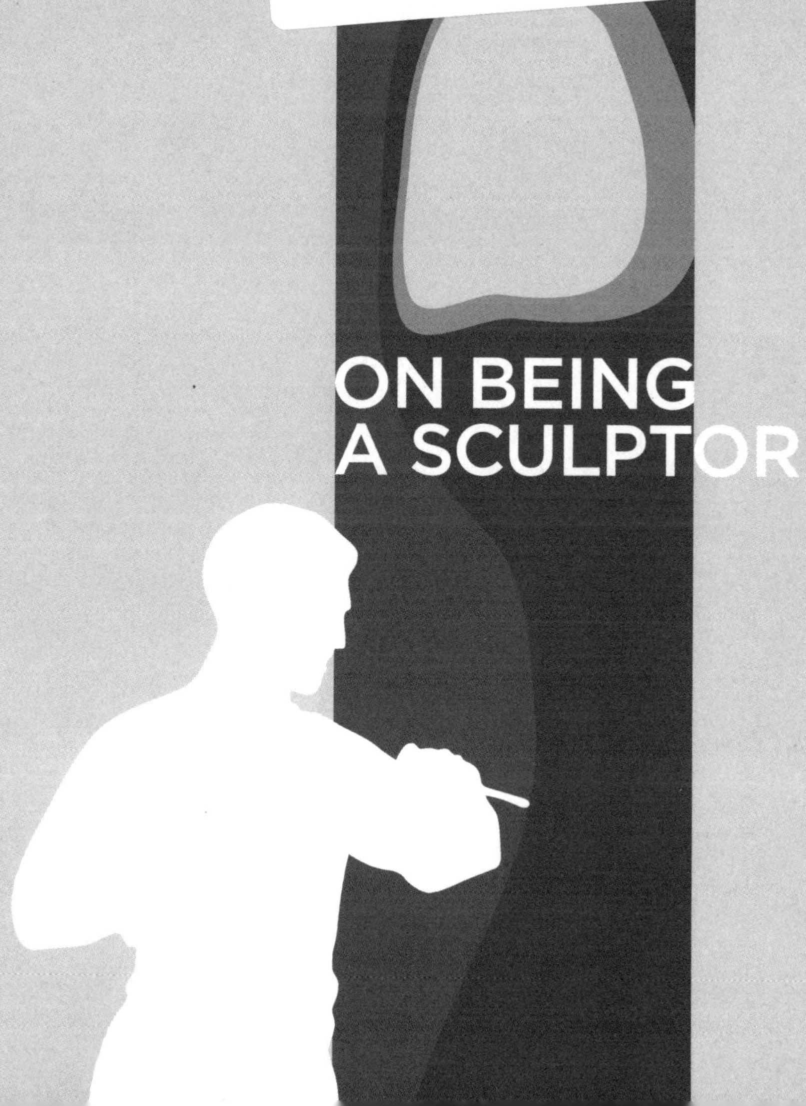

HENRY MOORE

ON BEING A SCULPTOR

TATE PUBLISHING

First published in 2010 by order of the Tate Trustees
by Tate Publishing, a division of Tate Enterprises Ltd,
Millbank, London SW1P 4RG
www.tate.org.uk/publishing

British Library Cataloguing in Publication Data
A catalogue record for this book is available
from the British Library
ISBN: 978 1 85437 906 1

Designed by Chalk

Reproduction by DL Interactive Ltd, London
Printed and bound by DZS Grafik, Slovenia

Printed on sustainably sourced, certified paper

Front cover: Henry Moore carving at No.3 Grove Studios, Adie Road, Hammersmith 1928 (detail)

CONTENTS

FOREV

MARY MOORE

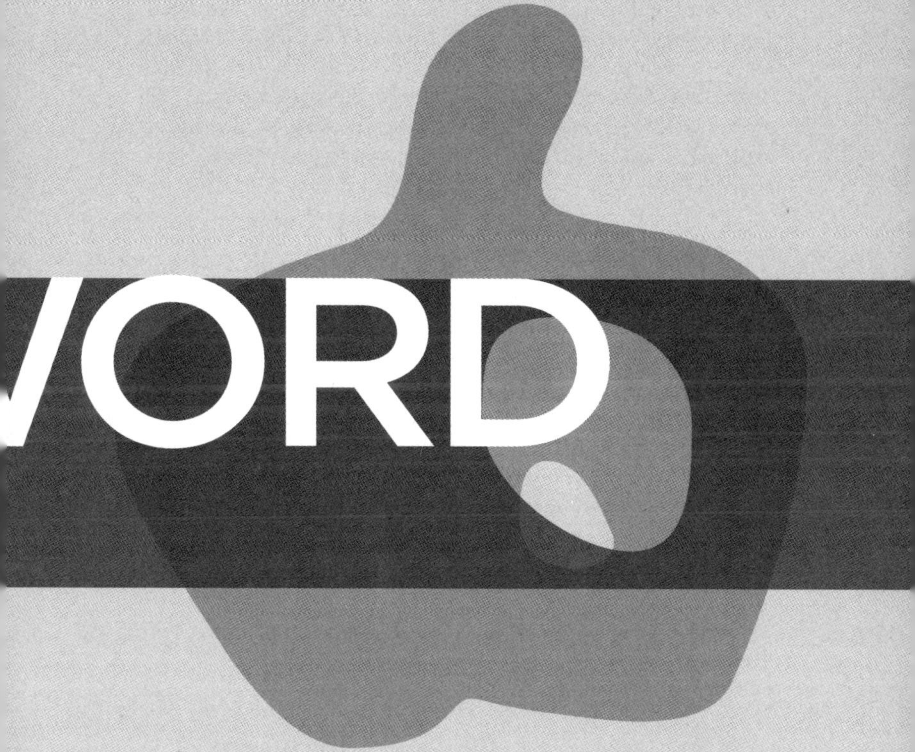
VORD

Though my father wrote in *The Listener* that it is a 'mistake for a sculptor or painter to speak or write very often about his job. It releases tension needed for his work', as Alan Wilkinson's edited collection of HM writing and conversations points out, contradictorily the Henry Moore bibliography lists 598 entries including books, letters, exhibition catalogues, newspaper articles, periodical articles, interviews, sound recordings, films, and videos.

Certainly, from a very early age I was keenly aware that communication was a vitally important part of my father's life, and therefore everyday family life. He took the most enormous time and care over writing anything, be it an article or just a letter. He even loved to scan the spelling and punctuation in my primary school essays. And we often played word games at lunch with the OED as referee. People came to our house all the time, from TV crews to architects, writers, world famous musicians, or just art students turning up, unannounced, on a bicycle. Our house was an open house. Astonishingly, the balance between the public and the private, the internal and the external, seemed to flow naturally and dynamically.

Without question, my father was a great communicator. It is often given that, of course he'd been a teacher, born into a family of teachers. But it also helped that he just loved people. He said that he could teach anyone to draw, but what he was really teaching was how to see. And how to see in a sculptural and three-dimensional way. In talking about 'form-blindness' in *The Listener* in 1937, he explains the difference between two-dimensional and three-dimensional appreciation:

> *Many more people are 'form-blind' than colour-blind. The child learning to see, first distinguishes only two-dimensional shape ... it has to develop (partly by means of touch) the ability to judge roughly three-dimensional distances. But having satisfied the requirements of practical necessity, most people go no farther. Though they may attain considerable accuracy in the perception of flat form, they do not make the further intellectual and emotional effort needed to comprehend form in its full spatial existence.*

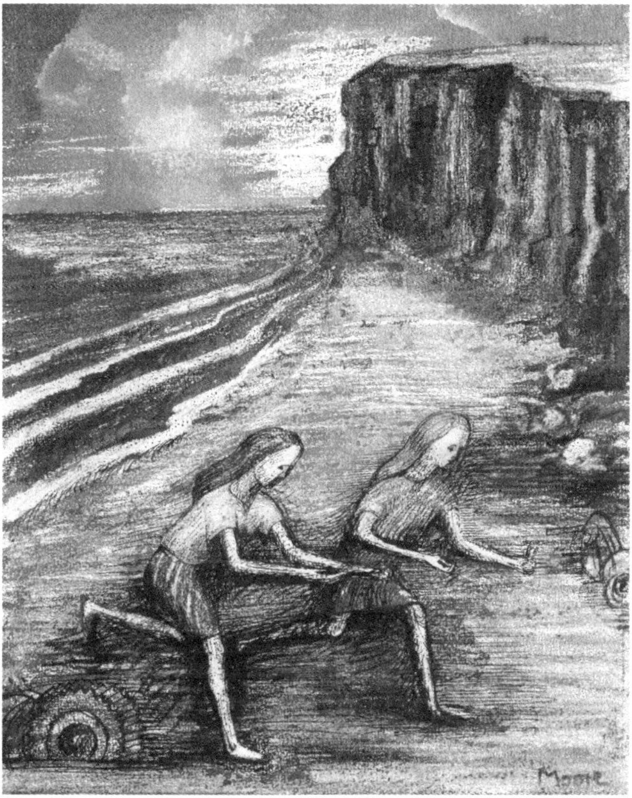

Henry Moore
***Illustration for a Poem by Herbert Read* 1946**
Pencil, wax crayon, charcoal, watercolour wash, pen and ink on paper
31.7 x 25.1 cm

Certainly, my childhood was a constant exposure to, 'the intellectual and emotional effort needed to comprehend form in its full spatial existence'. It pervaded every part of daily life, in and outside the studio. In the domestic arena, most strikingly in the form of games.

These games expanded and confirmed the three-dimensional experience: eccentric games of guessing the weight of my friends at my seventh birthday party, with the help of the bathroom scales; finding the centre of a piece of paper, drawing games with eyes tight shut (teaching me to internalise and draw from visual memory); having to visualise the back of something while you looked at the front.

We used to go to Broadstairs in Kent every summer, and stayed in a boarding house on the seafront, for two weeks. I suppose these holidays were a continuation of the way my parents had spent summers all their lives, but my father could only bear to take two weeks of holiday, as he couldn't tolerate being out of the studio for any longer. On these holidays, on rainy afternoons, and indeed frequently throughout the year, we'd play these familiar drawing games. The rock-pools on the beach were a source of discovery and we'd come back on the Tilbury Ferry with the car boot loaded with pebbles.

From a very early age I was aware of the importance of visual images. My father constantly photographed his own work. I also realised later, just how accessible this visual information was to me in the 1960s, compared with its availability to my father in his youth. In 'A View of Sculpture' he remarks on this development of modern communication and what an enormous impact it has had on the world view of sculpture. I was aware of how my father garnered images, for example his postcard collection. He bought postcards from every museum he visited and kept those sent by friends. His book collection and his visits to Zwemmer's bookshop, where, because he could not afford to buy, he almost memorised the contents of the books, and his sketchbooks filled with drawings, done in the British Museum or Musée de L'homme – these images were notes for an internalised vocabulary of form.

His collection of natural objects and pebbles too, had much the same function as his collection of books, postcards and sketchbooks. The idea that he took inspiration from these pebbles is misleading, rather they confirmed his own inner vocabulary (see 'The Sculptor Speaks'):

> *Sometimes for several years running I have been to the same part of the sea-shore – but each year a new shape of pebble has caught my eye, which the year before, though it was there in hundreds, I never saw. Out of the millions of pebbles passed in walking along the shore, I choose out to see with excitement only those, which fit in with my existing form-interest at the time.*

Sculptors make perfect fathers, particularly for daughters. They are physically able, immensely practical and inventive, and they can move huge chunks of stone. Above all they are emotionally intelligent and alert to their interior selves.

My father had a deep intuitive sense of how to access his subconscious and express it without allowing it to be distorted in the expression. The vocabulary he created allowed him to do that. His collection of, and internalising of, this visual imagery allowed him to create an everyman's vocabulary to express the subconscious. He often referred to this in his writing. *'I am very much aware that associational, psychological factors play a large part in sculpture. The meaning and significance of form itself probably depends on the countless associations of man's history'.* He never was overt in conversation, or didactic about this. Daily life was a constant journey to enlarge and discover ways of using and expressing this vocabulary.

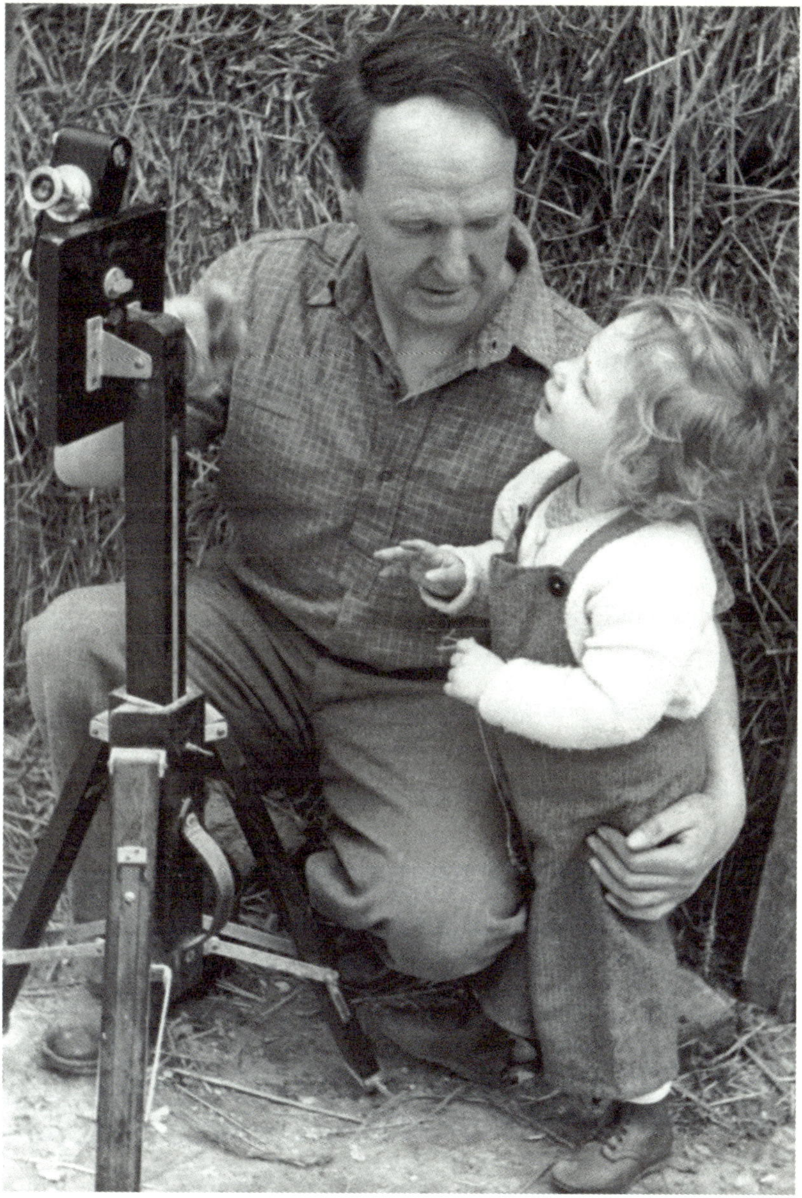

Henry Moore with his daughter
Mary at Perry Green c.1948

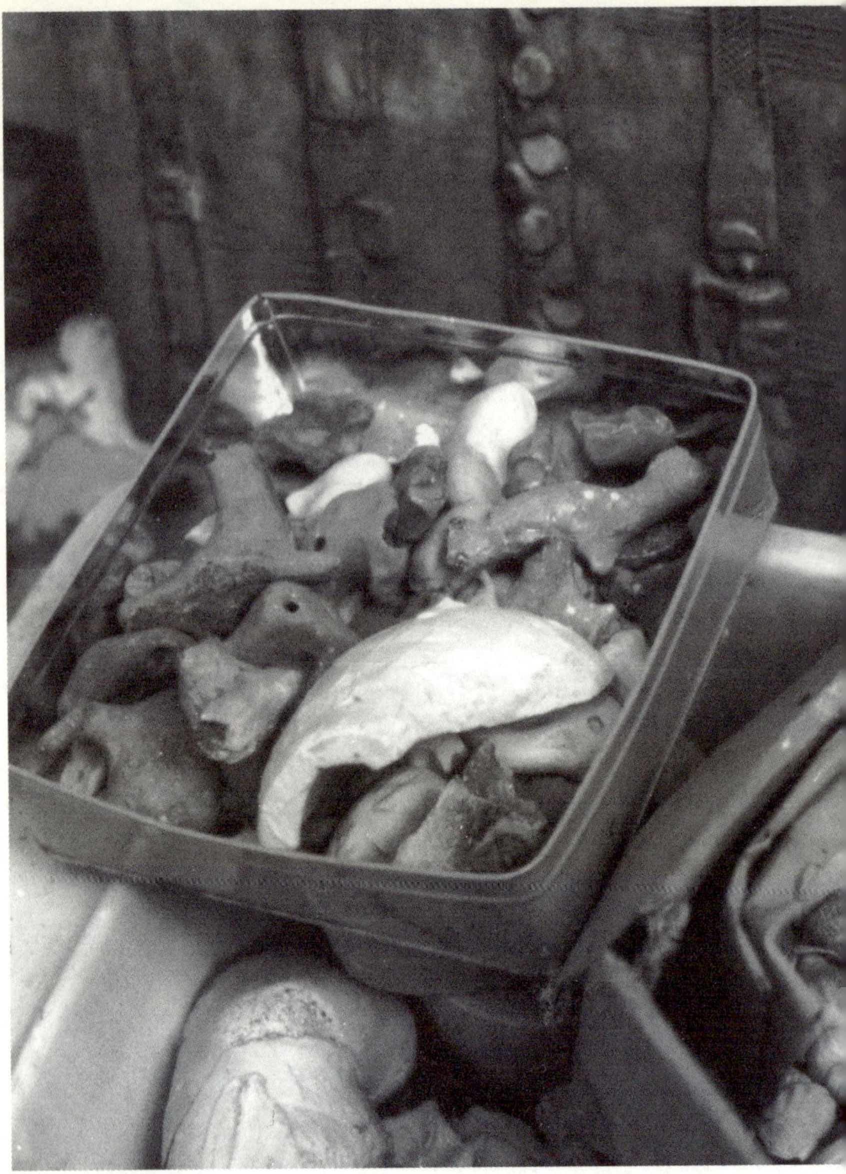

The floor of Moore's studio with a variety of boxes containing found objects.
In the background is *Plaster for Wall Relief: Maquette No.5* 1955

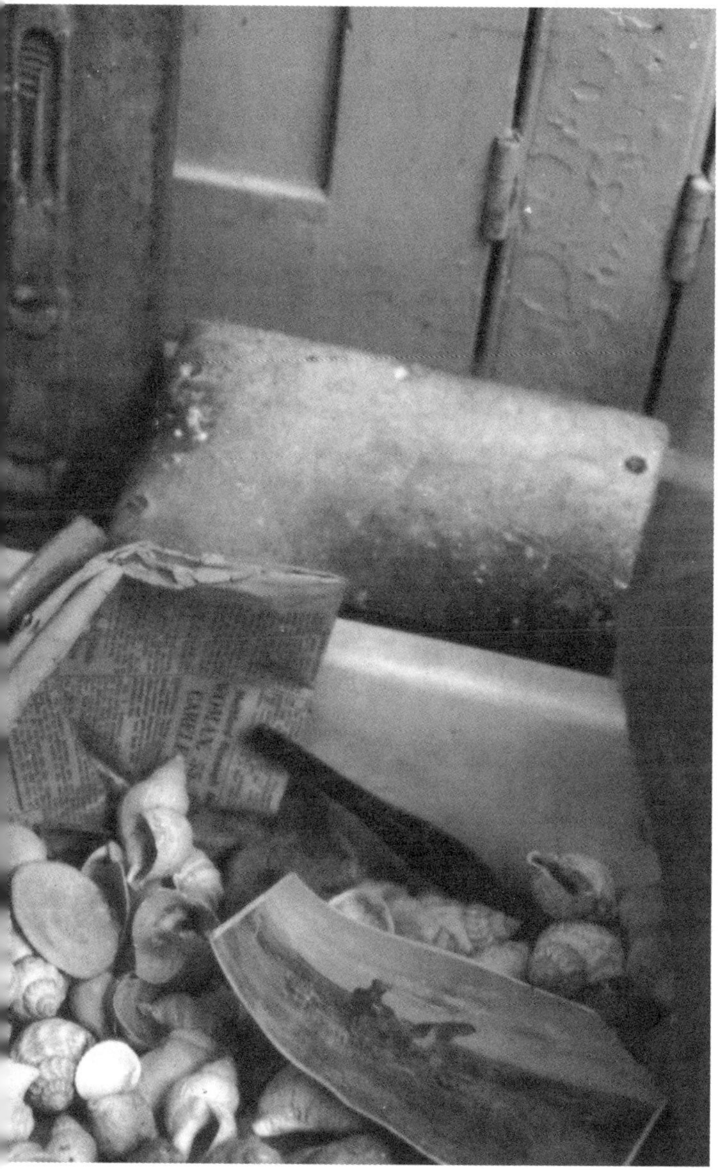

A VIEW
OF SCUL

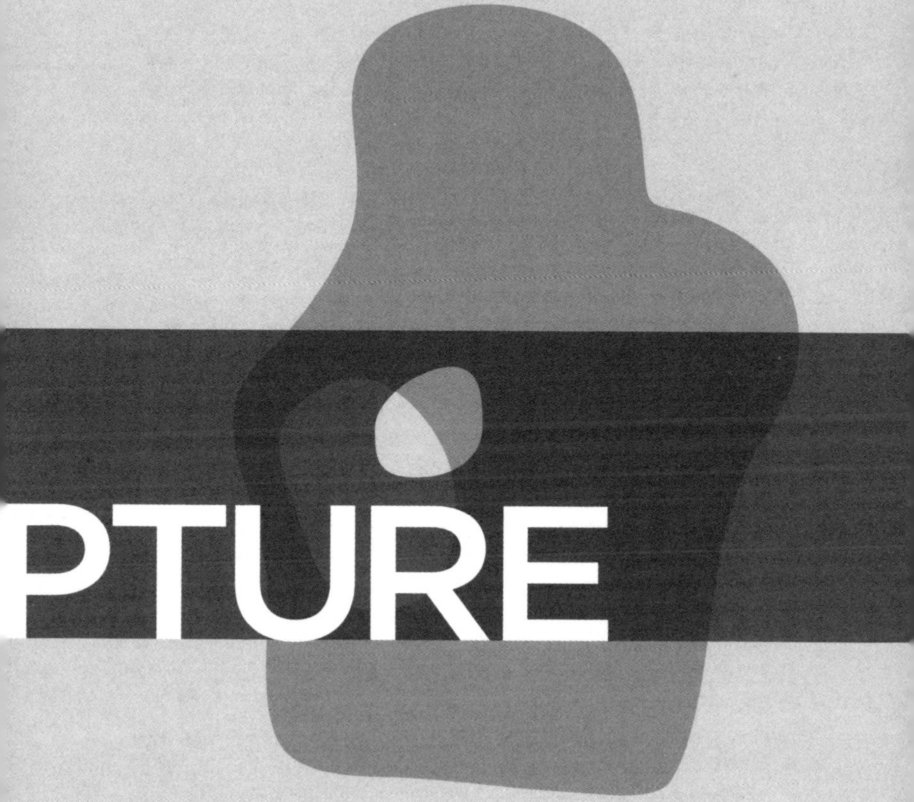
PTURE

In sculpture, the later Greeks worshipped their own likenesses, making realistic representation of much greater importance than it had been at any previous period. The Renaissance revived the Greek Ideal and European sculpture since then, until recent times, has been dominated by the Greek Ideal.

The world has been producing sculpture for at least some thirty thousand years. Through modern development of communication much of this we now know and the few sculptors of a hundred years or so of Greece no longer blot our eyes to the sculptural achievements of the rest of mankind. Palaeolithic and Neolithic sculpture, Sumerian, Babylonian and Egyptian, Early Greek, Chinese, Etruscan, Indian, Mayan, Mexican and Peruvian, Romanesque, Byzantine and Gothic, Negro, South Sea Island and North American Indian sculpture; actual examples or photographs of all are available, giving us a world view of sculpture never previously possible.

This removal of the Greek spectacles from the eyes of the modern sculptor (along with the direction given by the work of such painters as Cézanne and Seurat) has helped him to realise again the intrinsic emotional significance of shapes instead of seeing mainly a representation value, and freed him to recognise again the importance of the material in which he works, to think and create in his material by carving direct, understanding and being in sympathy with his material so that he does not force it beyond its natural constructive build, producing weakness; to know that sculpture in stone should look honestly like stone, that to make it look like flesh and blood, hair and dimples is coming down to the level of the stage conjurer.

A limitless scope is open to him. His inspiration will come, as always, from nature and the world around him, from which he learns such principles as balance, rhythm, organic growth of life, attraction and repulsion, harmony and contrast. His work may be comparatively representational or may be as Music and Architecture are, non-representational, but mechanical copying of objects and surrounding life will leave him dissatisfied - the Camera and Cameograph have nullified this as his aim. He will want his works to be creations, new in themselves, not merely feats of copying nor of memory, having only the second-hand life of realistic waxworks.

Each sculptor differs in his aims and ideals according to his different character, personality and his point of development. The sculpture which moves me most is full blooded and self-supporting, fully in the round, that is, its component forms are completely realised and work as masses in opposition, not being merely indicated by surface cutting in relief; it is not perfectly symmetrical, it is static and it is strong and vital, giving out something of the energy and power of great mountains. It has a life of its own, independent of the object it represents.

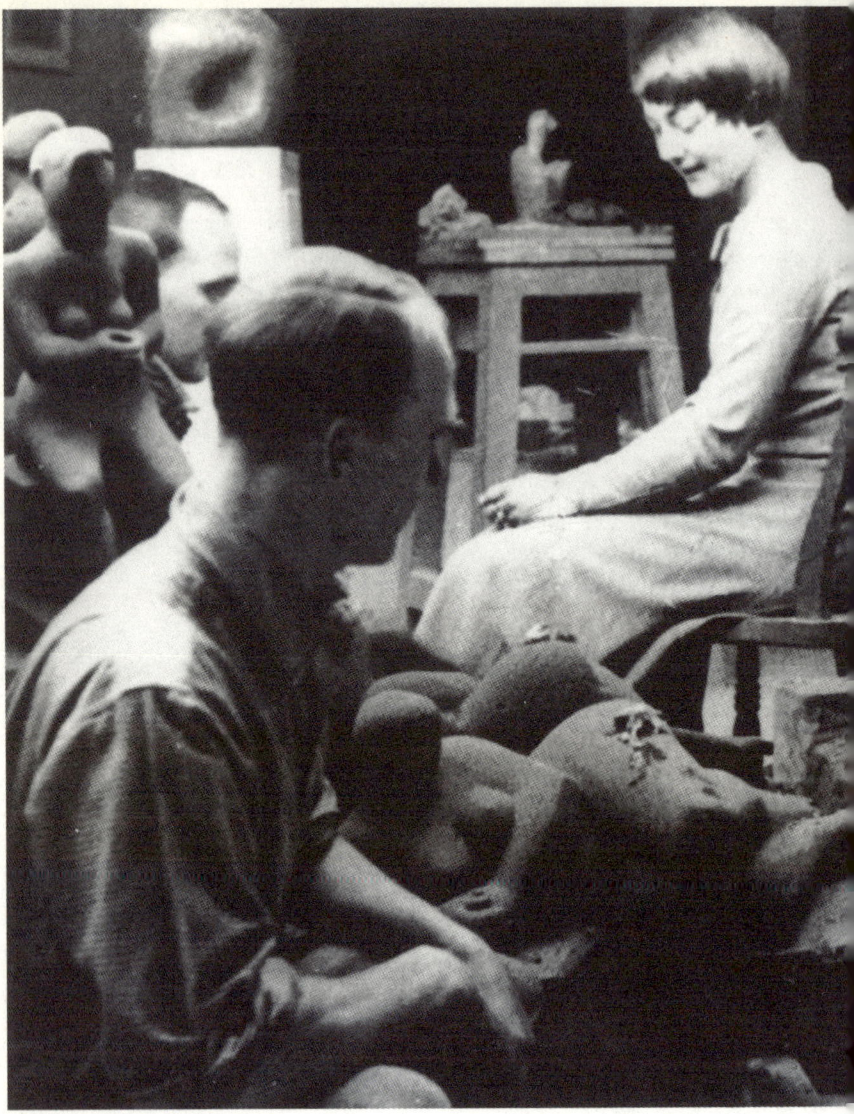

Henry and Irina Moore in
the Parkhill Road studio 1930

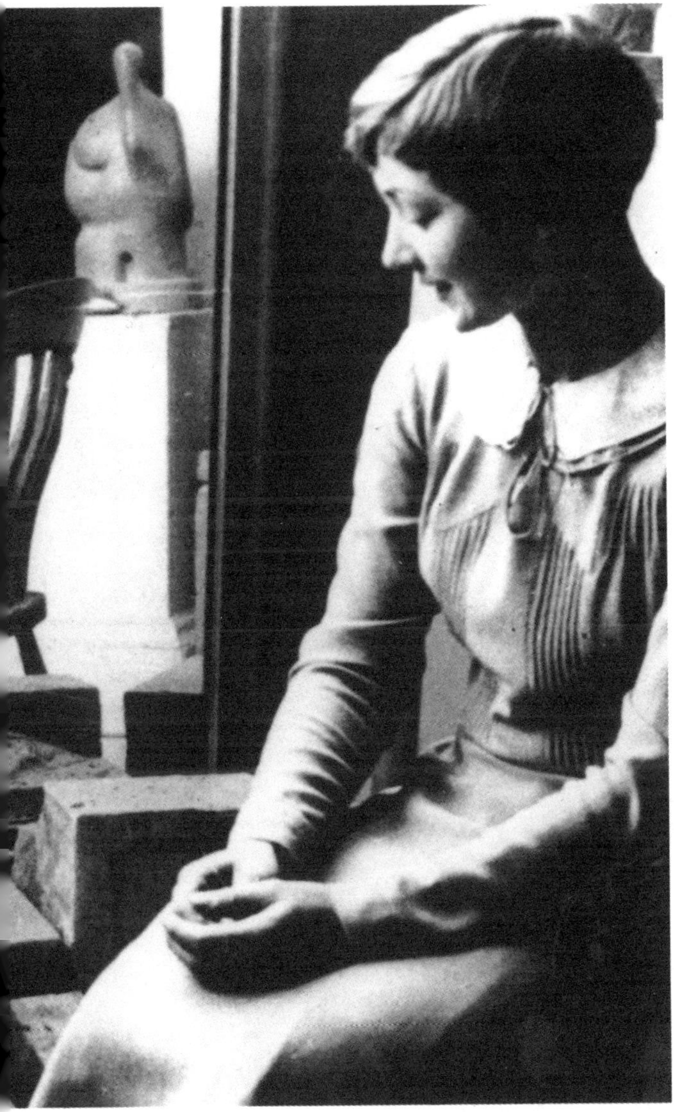

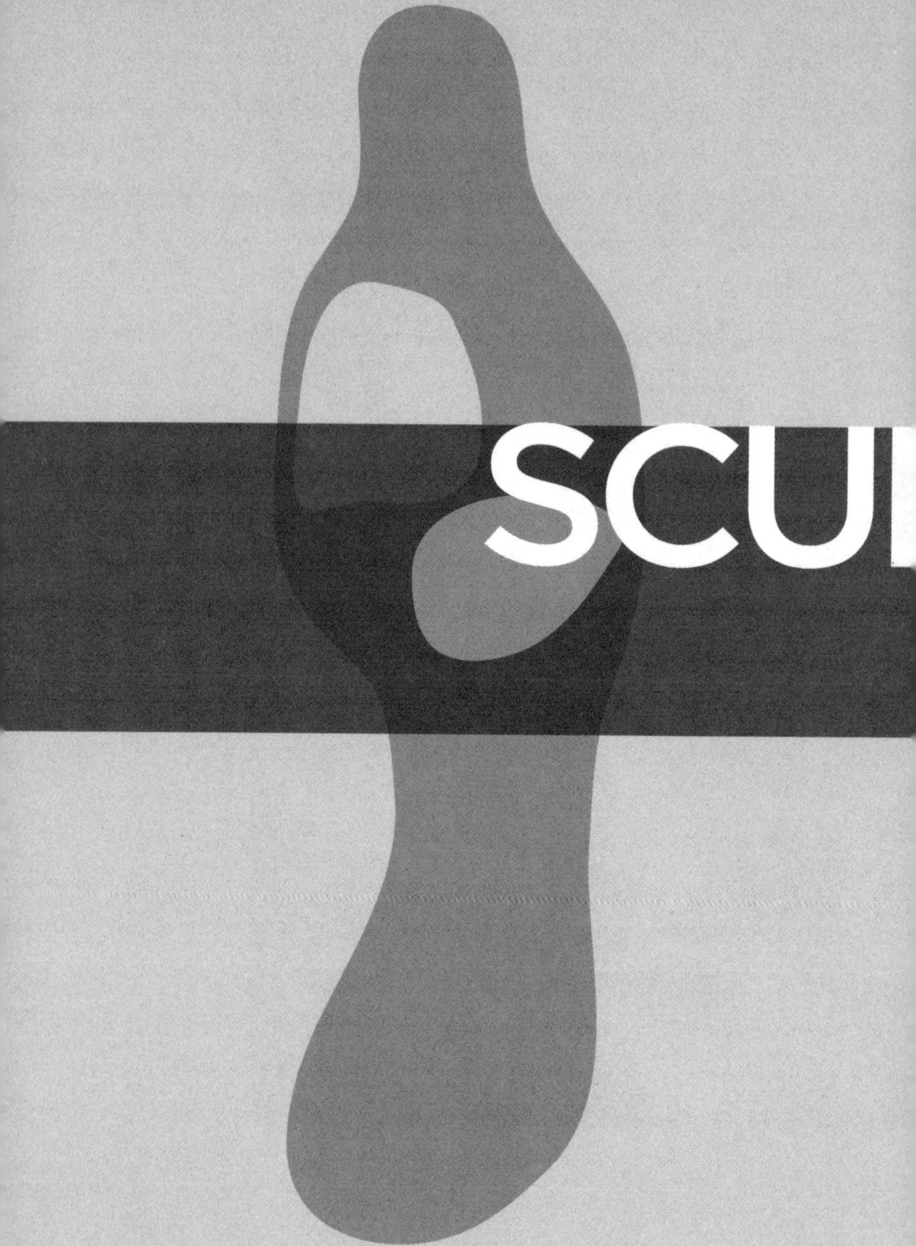
SCU

THE

LPTOR

SPEAKS

It is a mistake for a sculptor or a painter to speak or write very often about his job. It releases tension needed for his work. By trying to express his aims with rounded-off logical exactness, he can easily become a theorist whose actual work is only a caged-in exposition of conceptions evolved in terms of logic and words.

But though the non-logical, instinctive subconscious part of the mind must play its part in his work, he also has a conscious mind, which is not inactive. The artist works with a concentration of his whole personality, and the conscious part of it resolves conflicts, organises memories, and prevents him from trying to walk in two directions at the same time.

It is likely, then, that a sculptor can give, from his own conscious experience, clues which will help others in their approach to sculpture, and this article tries to do this and no more. It is not a general survey of sculpture, or of my own development, but a few notes on some of the problems that have concerned me from time to time.

Appreciation of sculpture depends on the ability to respond to form in three dimensions. That is perhaps why sculpture has been described as the most difficult of all arts; certainly it is more difficult than the arts which involve appreciation of flat forms, shape in only two dimensions. Many more people are 'form-blind' than colour-blind. The child learning to see, first distinguishes only two-dimensional shape; it cannot judge distances, depths. Later, for its personal safety and practical needs, it has to develop (partly by means of touch) the ability to judge roughly three dimensional distances. But having satisfied the requirements of practical necessity, most people go no farther. Though they may attain considerable accuracy in the perception of flat form, they do not make the further intellectual and emotional effort needed to comprehend form in its full spatial existence.

This is what the sculptor must do. He must strive continually to think of, and use, form in its full spatial completeness. He gets the solid shape, as it were, inside his head – he thinks of it, whatever its size, as if he were holding it completely enclosed in the hollow of his hand. He mentally visualises a complex form from all round itself; he knows while he looks at one side what the other side is like; he identifies himself with its centre of gravity, its mass, its weight; he realises its volume, as the space that the shape displaces in the air.

And the sensitive observer of sculpture must also learn to feel shape simply as shape, not as description or reminiscence. He must, for example, perceive an egg as a simple single solid shape, quite apart from its significance as food, or from the literary idea that it will become a bird. And so with solids such as a shell, a nut, a plum, a pear, a tadpole, a mushroom, a mountain peak, a kidney, a carrot, a tree-trunk, a bird, a bud, a lark, a lady-bird, a bulrush, a bone. From these he can go on to appreciate more complex forms or combinations of several forms.

Since the Gothic, European sculpture had become overgrown with moss, weeds – all sorts of surface excrescences which completely concealed shape. It has been Brancusi's special mission to get rid of this overgrowth, and to make us once more shape-conscious. To do this he has had to concentrate on very simple direct shapes, to keep his sculpture, as it were, one-cylindered, to refine and polish a single shape to a degree almost too precious. Brancusi's work, apart from its individual value, has been of historical importance in the development of contemporary sculpture. But it may now be no longer necessary to close down and restrict sculpture to the single (static) form unit. We can now begin to open out. To relate and combine together several forms of varied sizes, sections and directions into one organic whole.

Although it is the human figure which interests me most deeply, I have always paid great attention to natural forms, such as bones, shells, and pebbles, etc. Sometimes for several years running I have been to the same part of the sea-shore – but each year a new shape of pebble has caught my eye, which the year before, though it was there in hundreds, I never saw. Out of the millions of pebbles passed in walking along the shore, I choose out to see with excitement only those which fit in with my existing form-interest at the time. A different thing happens if I sit down and examine a handful one by one. I may then extend my form-experience more, by giving my mind time to be conditioned to a new shape.

There are universal shapes to which everybody is sub-consciously conditioned and to which they can respond if their conscious control does not shut them off.

Pebbles show nature's way of working stone. Some of the pebbles I pick up have holes right through them.

When first working direct in a hard and brittle material like stone, the lack of experience and great respect for the material, the fear of ill-treating it, too often result in relief surface carving, with no sculptural power.

But with more experience the completed work in stone can be kept within the limitations of its material, that is, not be weakened beyond its natural constructive build, and yet be turned from an inert mass into a composition which has a full form existence, with masses of varied sizes and sections working together in spatial relationship.

A piece of stone can have a hole through it and not be weakened – if the hole is of studied size, shape and direction. On the principle of the arch, it can remain just as strong.

The first hole made through a piece of stone is a revelation.

The hole connects one side to the other, making it immediately more three-dimensional.

A hole can itself have as much shape-meaning as a solid mass.

Sculpture in air is possible, where the stone contains only the whole, which is the intended and considered form.

The mystery of the whole – the mysterious fascination of caves in hillsides and cliffs.

There is a right physical size for every idea.

Pieces of good stone have stood about my studio for long periods, because though I've had ideas which would fit their proportions and materials perfectly, their size was wrong.

There is a size to scale not to do with its actual physical size, its measurements in feet and inches – but connected with vision.

A carving might be several times over life size and yet be petty and small in feeling – and a small carving only a few inches in height can give the feeling of huge size and monumental grandeur, because the vision behind it is big. Example, Michelangelo's drawings or a Masaccio madonna – and the Albert Memorial.

Yet actual physical size has an emotional meaning. We relate everything to our own size, and our emotional response to size is controlled by the fact that men on the average are between five and six feet high.

An exact model to 1/10 scale of Stonehenge, where the stones could be less than us, would lose all its impressiveness.

Sculpture is more affected by actual size considerations than painting. A painting is isolated by a frame from its surroundings (unless it serves just a decorative purpose) and so retains more easily its own imaginary scale.

If practical considerations allowed me, cost of material, of transport etc., I should like to work on large carvings more often than I do. The average in-between size does not disconnect an idea enough from prosaic everyday life. The very small or the very big takes on added size emotion.

Recently I have been working in the country, where, carving in the open air, I find sculpture more natural than in a London studio, but it needs bigger dimensions. A large piece of stone or wood placed almost anywhere at random in a field, orchard or garden immediately looks right and inspiring.

My drawings are done mainly as a help towards making sculpture – as a means of generating ideas for sculpture, tapping oneself for the initial idea; and as a way of sorting out ideas and developing them.

Also, sculpture compared with drawing is a slow means of expression, and I find drawing a useful outlet for ideas which there is not time enough to realise as sculpture. And I use drawing as a method of study and observation of natural forms (drawings from life, drawings of bones, shells etc.)

And sometimes I draw just for its own enjoyment.

Experience, though, has taught me that the difference there is between drawing and sculpture should not be forgotten. A sculptural idea which may be satisfactory as a drawing always needs some alteration when translated into sculpture.

At one time whenever I made drawings for sculpture I tried to give them as much the illusion of real sculpture as I could – that is, I drew by the method of illusion, of light falling on a solid subject. But now I find that carrying a drawing so far that it becomes a substitute for the sculpture, either weakens the desire to do the sculpture or is likely to make the sculpture only a dead realisation of the drawing.

I now leave a wider latitude in the interpretation of the drawings I make for sculpture, and draw often in line and flat tones without the light and shade illusion of three dimensions; but this does not mean that the vision behind the drawing in only two dimensional.

The violent quarrel between the abstractionists and the surrealists seems to me quite unnecessary. All good art has contained both abstract and surrealist elements, just as it has contained both classical and romantic elements – order and surprise, intellect and imagination, conscious and unconscious. Both sides of the artists's personality must play their part. And I think the first inception of a painting or a sculpture may begin from either end. As far as my own experience is concerned, I sometimes begin a drawing with no preconceived problem to solve, with only the desire to use pencil and paper, and make lines, tones and shapes with no conscious aim; but as my mind takes in what is so produced, a point arrives where some idea becomes conscious and crystallises, and then a control and ordering begin to take place.

Or sometimes I start with a set subject; or to solve, in a block of stone of known dimensions, a sculptural problem I've given myself, and then consciously attempt to build an ordered relationship of forms, which shall express my idea. But if the work is to be more than just a sculptural exercise, unexplainable jumps in the process of thought occur; and the imagination plays its part.

It might seem from what I have said of shape and form that I regard them as ends in themselves. Far from it. I am very much aware that associational, psychological factors play a large part in sculpture. The meaning and significance of form itself probably depends on the countless associations of man's history. For example, rounded forms convey an idea of fruitfulness, maturity, probably because the earth, women's breasts, and most fruits are rounded, and these shapes are important because they have this background in our habits of perception. I think the humanist organic element will always be for me of fundamental importance in sculpture, giving sculpture its vitality. Each particular carving I make takes on in my mind a human or occasionally animal, character and personality, and this personality controls its design and formal qualities, and makes me satisfied or dissatisfied with the work as it develops.

My own aim and direction seems to be consistent with these beliefs, though it does not depend upon them. My sculpture is becoming less representational, less an outward visual copy, and so what some people would call more abstract; but only because I believe that in this way I can present the human psychological content of my work with the greatest directness and intensity.

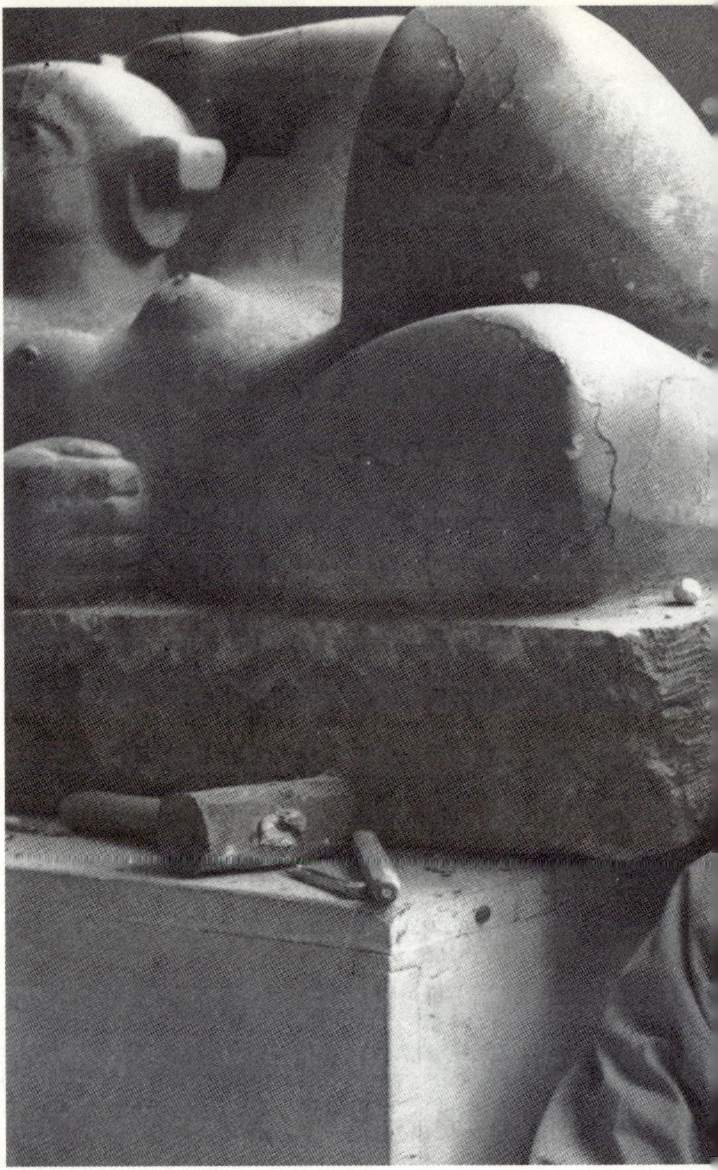

Moore in his Parkhill Road studio with
Reclining Figure (left) and *Standing Girl* c.1930

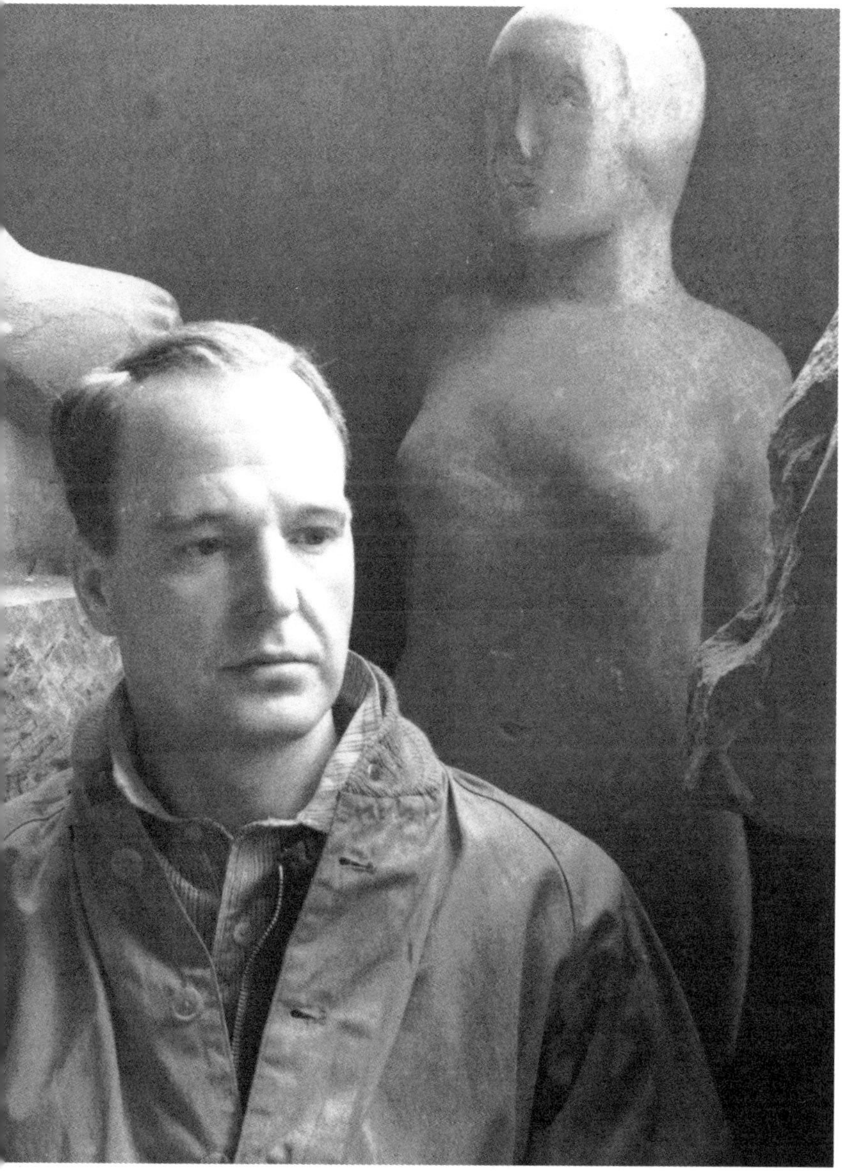

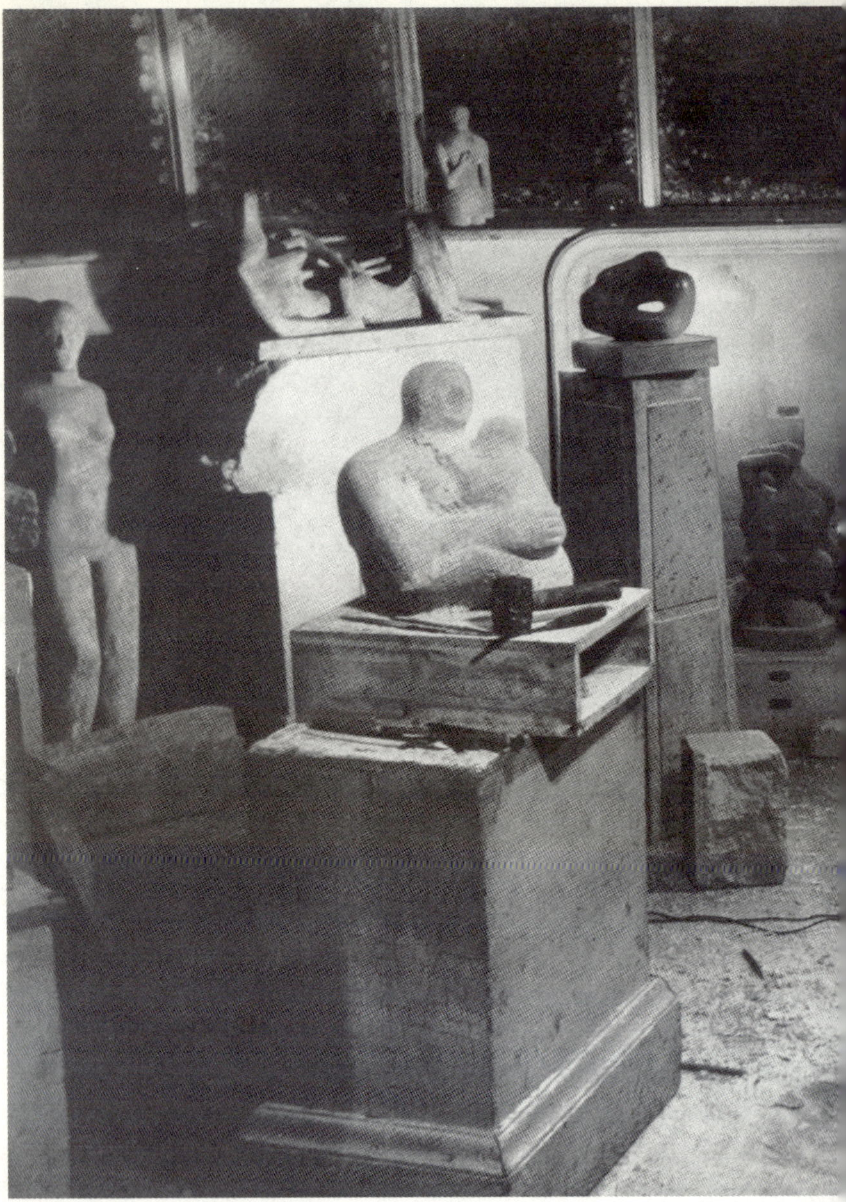

Henry Moore's studio at 11a Parkhill Road, Hampstead c.1933

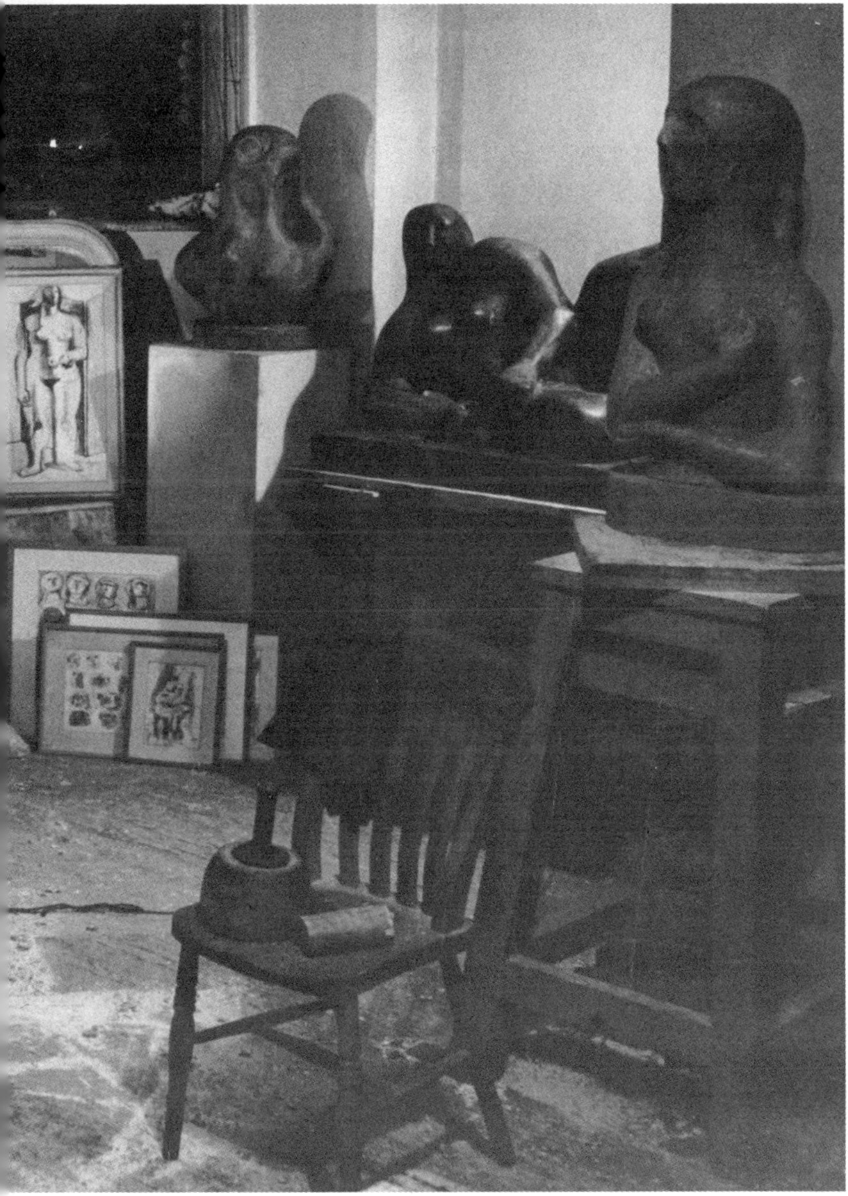

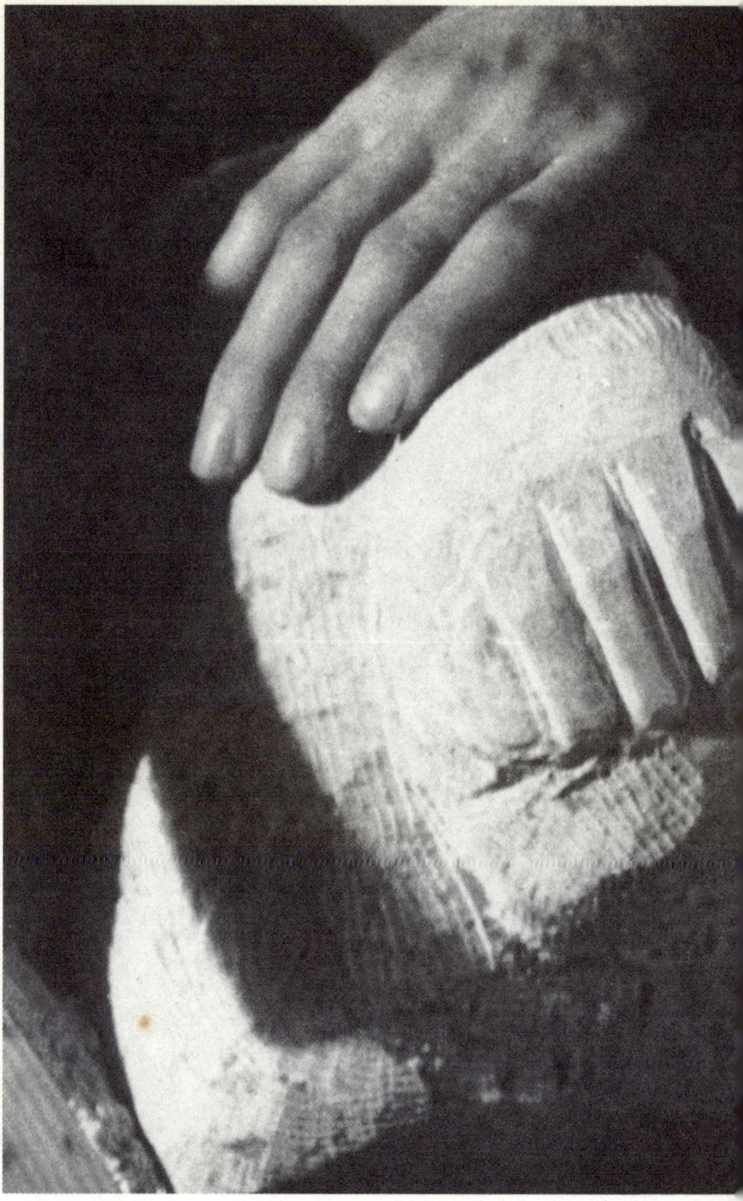

Moore holding an early carving, c.1930

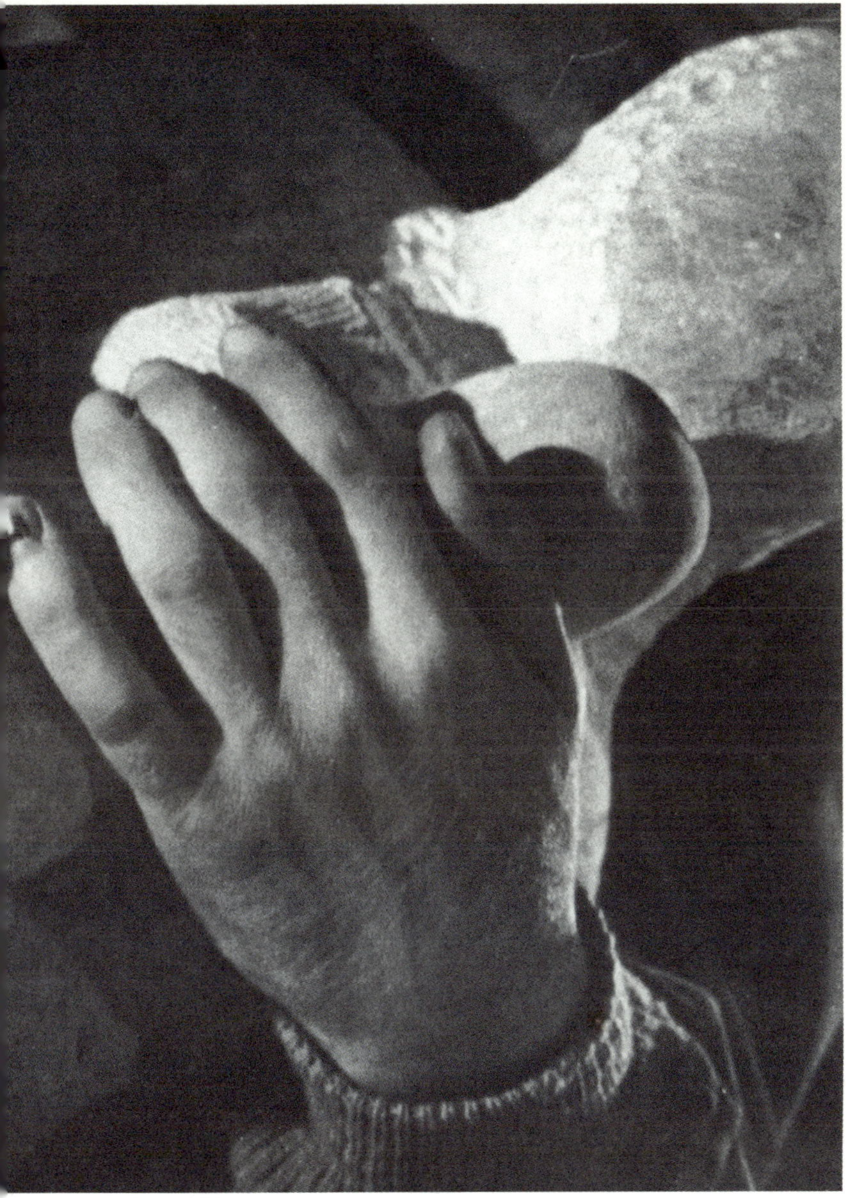

FROM

UNIT

ONE

Each sculptor through his past experience, through observation of natural laws, through criticism of his own work and other sculpture, through his character and psychological make-up, and according to his stage of development, finds that certain qualities in sculpture become of fundamental importance to him. For me these qualities are:

Truth to material

Every material has its own individual qualities. It is only when the sculptor works direct, when there is an active relationship with his material, that the material can take its part in the shaping of an idea. Stone, for example, is hard and concentrated and should not be falsified to look like soft flesh – it should not be forced beyond its constructive build to a point of weakness. It should keep its hard tense stoniness.

Full three-dimensional realisation

Complete sculptural expression is form in its full spatial reality.

Only to make relief shapes on the surface of the block is to forego the full power of expression of sculpture. When the sculptor understands his material, has a knowledge of its possibilities and its constructive build, it is possible to keep within its limitations and yet turn an inert block into a composition which has a full form-existence, with masses of varied size and section conceived in their air-surrounded entirety, stressing and straining, thrusting and opposing each other in spatial relationship – being static, in the sense that the centre of gravity lies within the base (and does not seem to be falling over or moving off its base) – and yet having an alert dynamic tension between its parts.

Sculpture fully in the round has no two points of view alike. The desire for form completely realised is connected with asymmetry. For a symmetrical mass being the same from both sides cannot have more than half the number of different points of view possessed by a non-symmetrical mass.

Asymetry is connected also with the desire for the organic (which I have) rather than the geometric.

Organic forms though they may be symmetrical in their main disposition, in their reaction to environment, growth and gravity, lose their perfect symmetry.

Observation of Natural Objects

The observation of nature is part of an artist's life, it enlarges his form-knowledge, keeps him fresh and from working only by formula, and feeds inspiration.

The human figure is what interests me most deeply, but I have found principles of form and rhythm from the study of natural objects such as pebbles, rocks, bones, trees, plants etc.

Pebbles and rocks show nature's way of working stone. Smooth, sea-worn pebbles show the wearing away, rubbed treatment of stone and principles of asymmetry.

Rocks show the hacked, hewn treatment of stone, and have a jagged nervous block rhythm.

Bones have marvellous structural strength and hard tenseness of form, subtle transition of one shape into the next and great variety in section.

Trees (tree trunks) show principles of growth and strength of joints, with easy passing of one section into the next. They give the ideal for wood sculpture, upward twisting movement.

Shells show nature's hard but hollow form (metal sculpture) and have a wonderful completeness of single shape.

There is in nature a limitless variety of shapes and rhythms (and the telescope and microscope have enlarged the field) from which the sculptor can enlarge his form-knowledge experience.

But besides formal qualities there are qualities of vision and expression.

Vision and expression
My aim in work is to combine as intensely as possible the abstract principles of sculpture along with the realisation of my idea.

All art is an abstraction to some degree (in sculpture the material alone forces one away from pure representation and towards abstraction).

Abstract qualities of design are essential to the value of a work, but to me of equal importance is the psychological, human element. If both abstract and human elements are welded together in a work, it must have a fuller, deeper meaning.

Vitality and power of expression
For me a work must first have a vitality of its own. I do not mean a reflection of the vitality of life, of movement, physical action, frisking, dancing figures and so on, but that a work can have in it a pent-up energy, an intense life of its own, independent of the object it may represent. When a work has this powerful vitality we do not connect the word Beauty with it.

Beauty, in the later Greek or Renaissance sense, is not the aim of my sculpture.

Between beauty of expression and power of expression there is a difference of function. The first aims at pleasing the senses, the second has a spiritual vitality which for me is more moving and goes deeper than the senses.

Because a work does not aim at reproducing natural appearances it is not, therefore, an escape from life – but may be a penetration into reality, not a sedative or drug, not just the exercise of good taste, the provision of pleasant shapes and colours in a pleasing combination, not a decoration to life, but an expression of the significance of life, a stimulation to a greater effort in living.

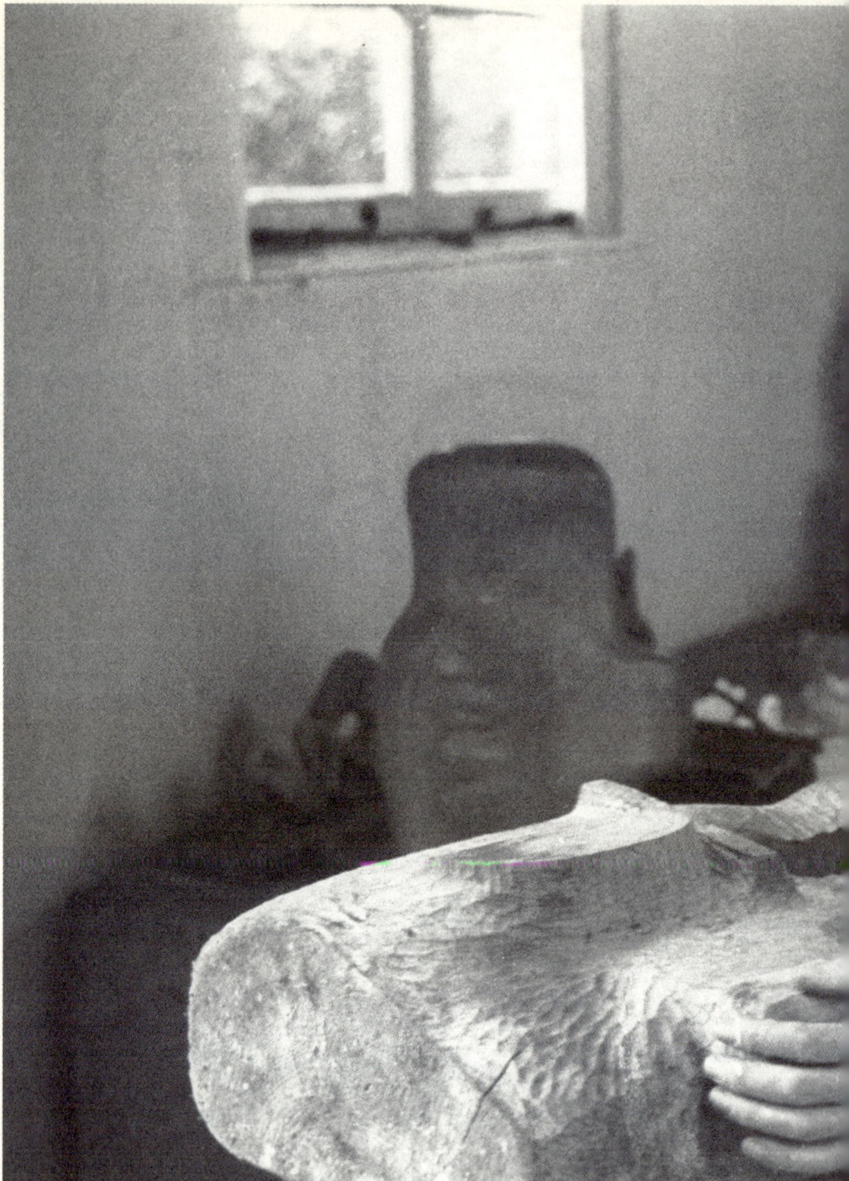

Moore carving *Family* in his studio at Perry Green 1935

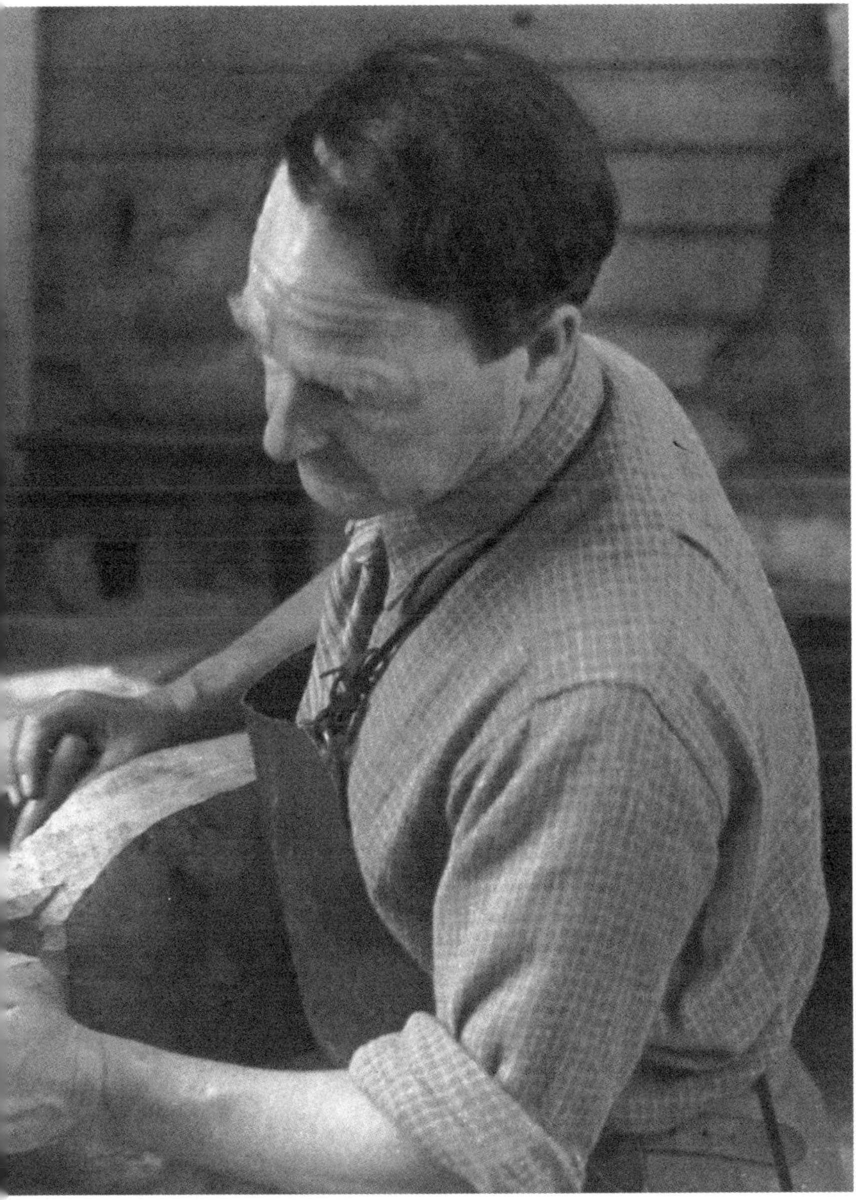

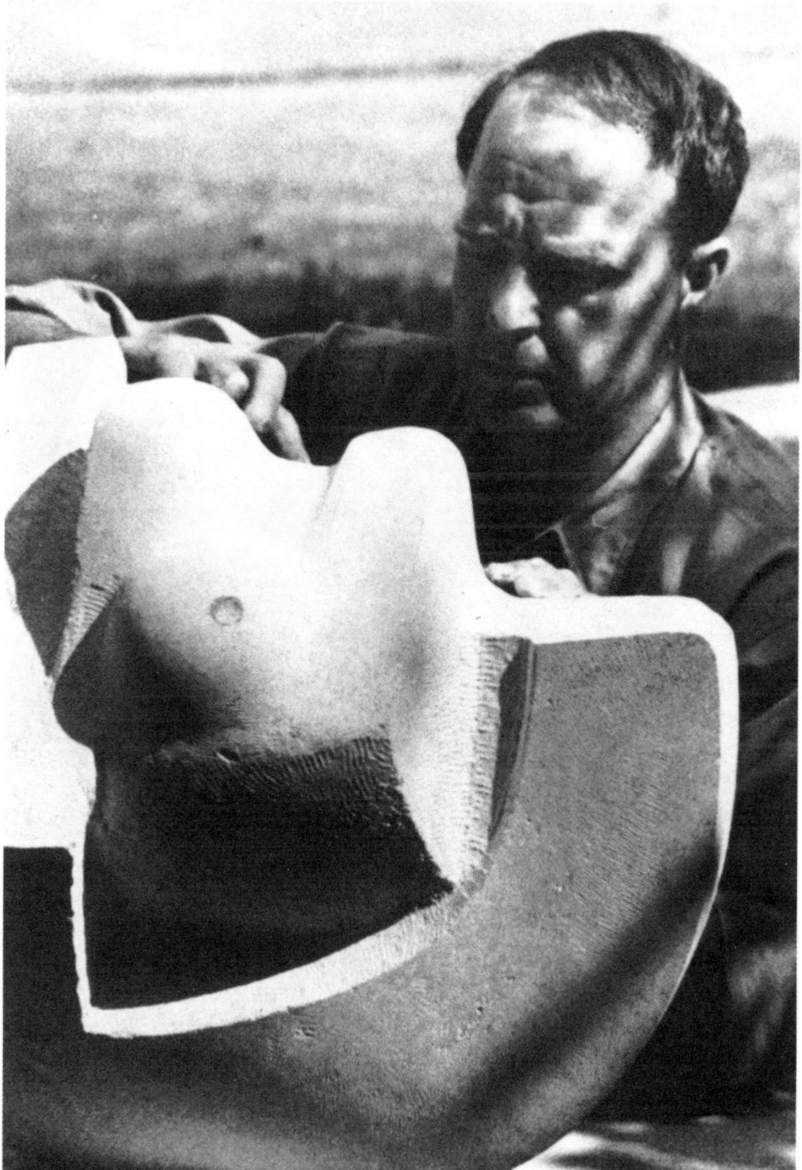

Moore working on the Hopton wood carving *Sculpture* 1937, Burcroft, Kent

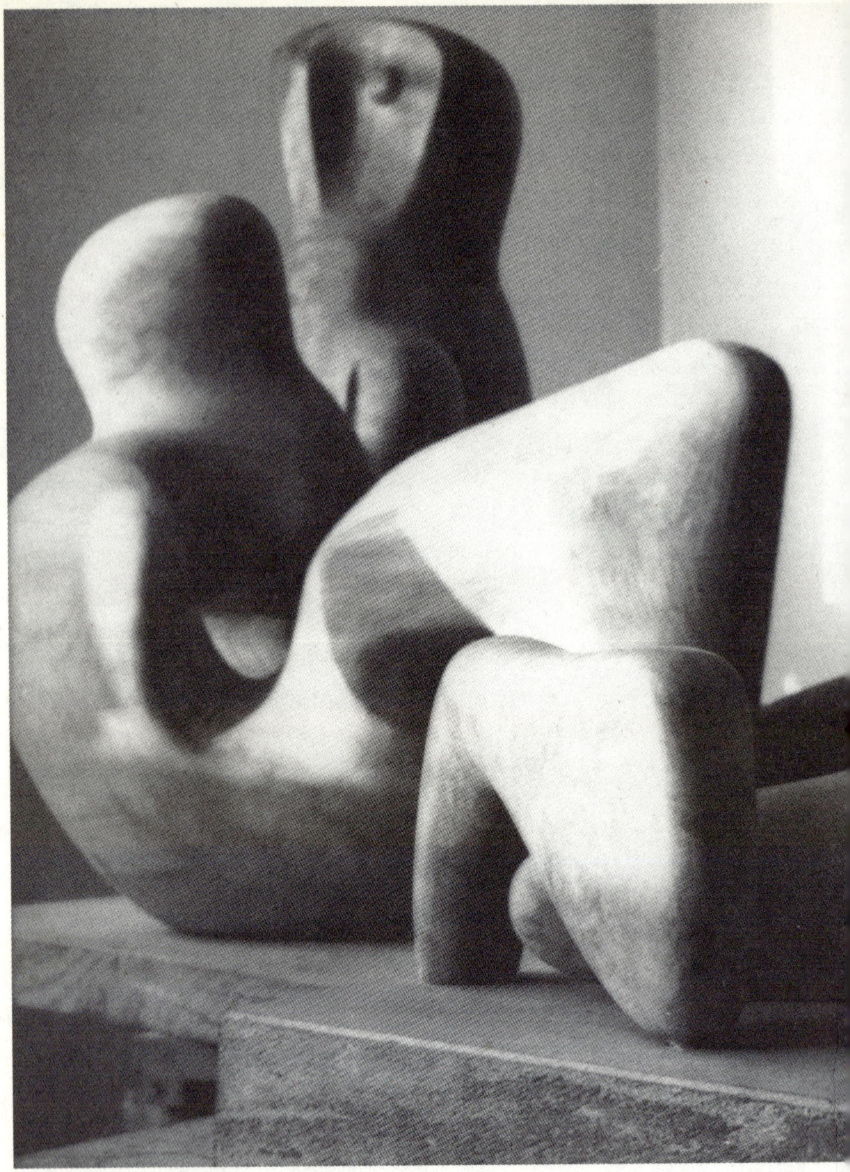

A group of sculptures with Four-piece Composition: *Reclining Figure* (centre) in Moore's studio at 11A Parkhill Road, c.1935

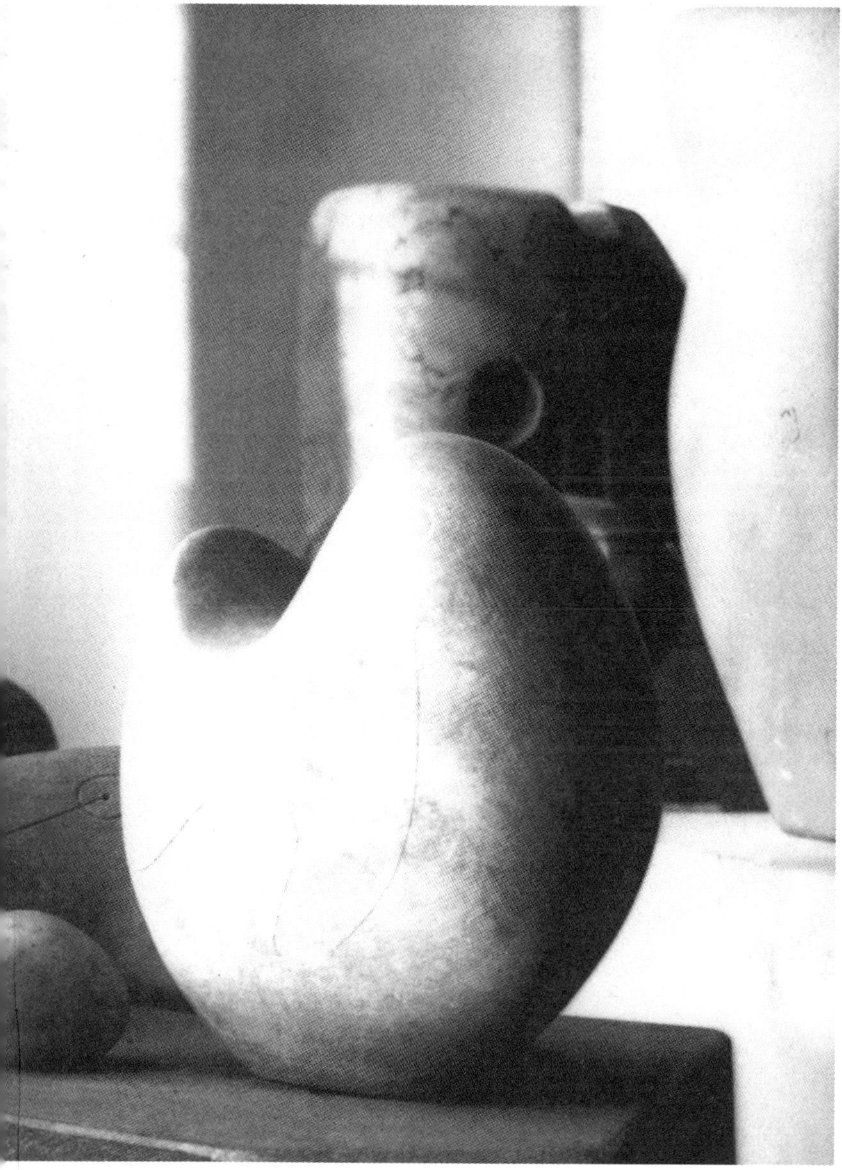

Credits

'A View of Sculpture' (pp.18–19) was headed 'Contemporary English Sculptors: Henry Moore' when first published in the *Architectural Association Journal* in May 1930. It was given the title 'A View of Sculpture' when republished in 1957 in the fourth edition of *Sculpture and Drawings 1921–1948*.

'The Sculptor Speaks' (pp.24–5) appeared in *The Listener*, vol. XVIII, No. 449, 18th August 1937, pp.338–40, London 1937.

The text from *Unit One* (pp. 38–40) was first published in *Unit One*, ed. Herbert Read, London 1934.

Photocredits

p.34: Thea Struve